# Curly and Straight

Written by: Mya Barr

Illustrated by: Felicia Leavesly

*For my parents-*
*my role models and biggest supporters.*

It was the first day of Kindergarten.

Mara woke up with butterflies in her stomach.

Mya woke up buzzing with excitement!

Mara's mom tried to tame her hair.

Mya's mom put her hair in a ponytail.

Mara ate toast topped with strawberry jelly for breakfast.

Mya ate waffles and filled each hole with syrup!

Mara dashed out of the house!

"Goodbye, Coco!"

Mya danced out the door.

"See ya later, Millie!"

They both arrived early
and ran to the swing set.

"Hi, I'm Mya," said the girl with straight black hair.

"Hi, I'm Mara," said the girl with curly blonde hair.

Mya introduced herself.
"I like pink, elephants and music!"

She enjoyed playing
dress up and reading.

Mara followed, "Hmm. My favorites are blue, rhinos, and soccer..."

She much preferred playing on her Gameboy and math.

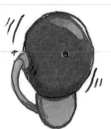

*Riiiiing*

Happy to have a new friend,
the opposite girls ran inside!

"Welcome class!" – Ms.
Zindler smiled.

After an introduction
to Kindergarten...

They painted
together in art..

They played
hide and seek...

They swung
from the
monkey bars...

And learned
how to type!

33

Ms. Zindler then
started storytime.

"Mya! I mean Mara,
will you please pick a book?"

Ms. Zindler then led song.

"Mara! I mean, Mya, will you please pass out the lyrics?"

Days went on and Ms. Zindler continued to get their names mixed up... They were always together!

"Mya! I mean, Mara..."

"Mara? Oops! I mean, Mya..."

This happened everyday!

One day, she finally said:

"Okay, that's it! I'll call YOU
"Curly" and YOU "Straight!"

The girls looked at each other, with
big smiles on their faces, and giggled.

Who knew that two strangers
could become friends in
just a few short days!

Curly and Straight in real life!

Curly and Straight

iUniverse books may be ordered through booksellers or by contacting:

iUniverse
1663 Liberty Drive
Bloomington, IN 47403
www.iuniverse.com
844-349-9409

ISBN: 978-1-6632-2948-9 (sc)
978-1-6632-2949-6 (e)

Library of Congress Control Number: 2021919658

Print information available on the last page.

iUniverse rev. date:  09/28/2021

Printed in the United States
by Baker & Taylor Publisher Services